PREFACE

This report sets forth the statutes, Executive Branch documents, regulations, and Department of Defense (DoD) internal directives that define and govern Military Support to Civil Authorities (MSCA). The policies and responsibilities of the military departments and staff agencies of DoD are reviewed, as they have evolved from the early 1950s to the present. The events of September 11, 2001, have placed the MSCA function in the larger context of homeland security, and documents setting forth homeland security policy as it defines MSCA have been reviewed as well. This report also discusses DoD civilian and military responsibility for MSCA, and the states' position regarding the National Guard's role in support of civil authorities. Finally, this report evaluates the criteria for providing MSCA, and assesses how DoD compares this function with its warfighting mission.

I0448687

TABLE OF CONTENTS

INTRODUCTION

The U.S. military has provided support to civil authorities in response to civil emergencies and natural disasters dating back to the Truman era. The terminology applied to this function has varied over the years: military assistance, or military support to civil authorities; military support of civil defense; and employment of military resources in natural disaster emergencies within the United States. As will be illustrated in this report's discussion of U.S. Defense Department (DoD) regulatory documents, the specific responsibilities of the department and the service branches were initially divided between civil defense (attacks on the United States) and disaster-related civil emergencies, but now are addressed collectively as Military Support to Civil Authorities (MSCA) as a matter of departmental policy and doctrine. In addition, the events of September 11, 2001, and the subsequent creation of a homeland security infrastructure have resulted in the adoption of MSCA policy in the context of the broader issue of homeland defense. However, both the core regulations and the DoD internal directive that govern MSCA predate the post–9/11 world, because they were adopted in 1993. In addition, the primary statutory authority for these documents is the Federal Civil Defense Act of 1950, which was repealed in 1994. Consequently, all of the recent policy statements defining MSCA and establishing DoD's role are found in homeland security directives and strategy documents issued by the White House and the military.

The U.S. Department of Defense, in its 2005 *Strategy for Homeland Defense and Civil Support*, defines defense support of civil authorities as "DoD support, including Federal military forces, the Department's career civilian and contractor personnel, and DoD agency and component assets, for domestic emergencies and for designated law enforcement and other activities." This function is provided when DoD is directed to do so by the president or the secretary of defense.[1] A report on the future of the National Guard and Reserves issued in 2006 defines "civil support" as "an umbrella term that encompasses the support the Department of Defense could provide as part of a response to a natural disaster or terrorist attack, to include an event involving chemical, biological, nuclear, radiological, or explosive materials (CBRNE), as

---

[1] U.S. Department of Defense, *Strategy for Homeland Defense and Civil Support*, June 2005, 5, http://www.defense link.mil/news/Jun2005/d20050630homeland.pdf.

well as support DoD could provide for other law enforcement activities."[2] DoD's *Homeland Security* doctrine issued by the Joint Chiefs of Staff in August 2005 states "MSCA is the most widely recognized form of DOD Civil Support because it usually consists of support for high-profile emergencies such as natural or manmade disasters that often invoke Presidential or state emergency/disaster declarations. DOD assistance should be requested by an LFA (Lead Federal Agency) only when other local, state and federal capabilities have been exhausted or when a military-unique capability is required."[3] MSCA is generally provided during natural disasters, special security events, and accidental or intentional manmade disasters that have evoked a presidential or state emergency declaration.[4] Major Robert Preiss, a former strategic analyst in the National Guard Bureau, defined MSCA in 2003 as "assistance to civilian governmental entities – Federal, state, or local – that the services may provide to help manage a crisis, attack, or calamity."[5] The *National Response Plan* issued by the Department of Homeland Security in December 2004, which is discussed in greater detail in a separate section of this report, also stipulates that DoD civil support is generally provided only when local, state and other federal resources are "overwhelmed."[6]

The National Guard is considered a unique state-based military force (although primarily funded by the federal government and trained in accordance with federal standards) that is the "only military force shared by the states and the federal government."[7] According to National Guard Bureau Chief H. Steven Blum, the Guard's "unique ability to work in three legal statuses makes the Guard the most versatile DOD force available to the Federal Government for homeland security (HLS), homeland defense (HD), and military assistance to civil authorities (MACA)."[8] The three statuses Lt. General Blum refers to are:

---

[2] Christine Wormuth, *The Future of the National Guard and Reserves: The Beyond Goldwater-Nichols Phase III Report* (Washington, DC: Center for Strategic and International Studies, July 2006), 62, http://www.csis.org/media/csis/pubs/bgn_ph3_report.pdf.

[3] U.S. Joint Chiefs of Staff, *Homeland Security*, Joint Publication 3–26, August 2, 2005, IV–4, http://www.dtic.mil/doctrine/jel/new_pubs/jp3_26.pdf.

[4] U.S. Library of Congress, Congressional Research Service, Washington, DC, *Hurricane Katrina: DOD Disaster Response*, September 19, 2005, RL 33095, CRS-2.

[5] Robert A. Priess, "The National Guard and Homeland Defense," *Joint Force Quarterly*, no.36 (2003): 72, http://www.ngb.army.mil/media/transcripts/preiss_jfq_36_article.pdf.

[6] U.S. Department of Homeland Security, *National Response Plan,* December 2004, 42, http://www.dhs.gov/xlibrary/assets/NRP_FullText.pdf.

[7] Timothy J. Lowenberg, "The Role of the National Guard in National Defense and Homeland Security," *National Guard*, September 1, 2005, 1, http://www.ngaus.org.

[8] H. Steven Blum, "A Vision for the National Guard," *Joint Force Quarterly*, no.36 (2003): 26.

- State active duty—States employ their National Guard forces under state control for state purposes and at state expense; command and control rests with the governor.

- Title 32 duty—Under authority of Title 32 of the U.S. Code, the National Guard is federally funded but under the command and control of the state's governor even though the Guard is employed "in the service of the United States." The purpose of the service may be either shared state/federal or for a primary federal purpose.

- Title 10 duty—Under authority of Title 10 of the U.S. Code, the National Guard is deployed by the President for a federal purpose; command and control rests solely with the President and the federal government.[9]

FRAMEWORK FOR MSCA AUTHORITY IN STATUTE AND EXECUTIVE-BRANCH DOCUMENTS

On December 1, 1950, by authority of Executive Order 10186, President Harry S. Truman established the Federal Civil Defense Administration and requested legislation providing statutory authority for the agency. One month later, Congress enacted Pub.L.No. 81–920, the Federal Civil Defense Act of 1950. This law, until its repeal in 1994 by Pub.L.No. 103–337, the National Defense Authorization Act for Fiscal Year 1995, provided primary statutory authority for MSCA regulations (Title 32, Code of Federal Regulations, Part 185). Other disaster relief statutes enacted over time also provided authority for the internal DoD directives governing military support/assistance to civil authorities and military support to civil defense (see below, DoD regulatory documents). In 1994 the Robert T. Stafford Disaster Relief and Emergency Assistance Act, Pub.L.No. 93–288, was enacted. As amended and codified at 42 U.S.C. 5121 et seq this law is the primary authority enabling DoD to engage in domestic consequence management operations.[10] In 2004 Congress amended Title 32 of the U.S. Code to provide clear statutory authority for the use of National Guard forces in support of homeland defense activities.

Federal Civil Defense Act of 1950

As enacted on January 12, 1951 and amended through 1981, the Federal Civil Defense Act of 1950 states the intent and policy of Congress to be the provision of "a system of civil defense for the protection of life and property in the United States from attack and from natural

---

[9] Lowenberg, 2–3.
[10] U.S. Northern Command, Joint Task Force Civil Support, http://www.htfcs.northcom.mil/pages/legalbasis.

disaster."[11] This responsibility for civil defense is "vested jointly in the Federal Government and the several states and their political subdivisions." The federal government is to provide "necessary direction, coordination, and guidance."[12] The president or Congress, by concurrent resolution, may proclaim a state of civil emergency if a determination is made that an enemy attack has caused or may cause substantial injury to civilian property or persons. During this period of emergency, the president is authorized to "direct, after taking into consideration the military requirements of the Department of Defense, and Federal department or agency to provide" personnel, materials, and facilities to aid the states, as well as emergency shelter.[13]

Other Disaster Relief Laws

A few months before passage of the Federal Civil Defense Act of 1950, Congress enacted Pub.L.No. 81–875, the intent of which was to provide "an orderly and continuing means of assistance by the Federal Government to the States and local governments in carrying out their responsibilities to alleviate suffering and damage resulting from major disasters." Major disasters were defined as floods, droughts, fires, hurricanes, earthquakes, storms, or other catastrophes.[14] This law was repealed by Pub.L.No. 91–606, the Disaster Relief Act of 1970. It is the intent of Pub.L.No. 91–606 to enable the federal government to assist state and local governments in carrying out relief efforts in times of major disasters by broadening the scope of existing major disaster relief programs; encouraging states to develop comprehensive relief plans; and better coordinating federal disaster relief programs.[15] Federal agencies are authorized, as directed by the president, to provide equipment, supplies, facilities and personnel to states and local governments.[16]

Robert T. Stafford Disaster Relief and Emergency Assistance Act

The Robert T. Stafford Disaster Relief and Emergency Assistance Act, Pub.L.No. 93–288 as amended (42 U.S.C. 5121 et seq) further expands federal disaster relief programs to assist

---

[11] 50 U.S.C. app.2251 et seq, Pub. Law No. 81–920, 64 Stat 1245, ch. 1228, January 12, 1951.
[12] 64 Stat 1246.
[13] 64 Stat 1252.
[14] Pub.L.No. 81–875, 64 Stat 1109, ch. 1125, September 30, 1950.
[15] Pub.L.No. 91–606, 84 Stat 1744, December 31, 1970.
[16] 84 Stat 1747.

state and local governments in carrying out their responsibilities in response to major disasters, i.e., natural catastrophes. Federal agencies are directed to use their statutory authorities and resources (including personnel, equipment, supplies, facilities, and managerial, technical, and advisory services) in support of state and local assistance efforts. Subchapter IV of this law— "major disaster assistance programs"—provides that "Federal agencies may on the direction of the President, provide assistance essential to meeting immediate threats to life and property resulting from a major disaster."[17] Regarding the "utilization of DOD resources," the law stipulates as a general rule:

> During the immediate aftermath of an incident which may ultimately qualify for assistance under … this Act, the Governor of the State in which such incident occurred may request the President to direct the Secretary of Defense to utilize the resources of the Department of Defense for the purpose of performing on public and private lands any emergency work which is made necessary by such incident and which is essential for the preservation of life and property. Such emergency work may only be carried out for a period not to exceed 10 days.[18]

National Guard Homeland Defense Activities

In 2003 Senator Diane Feinstein (D-CA) and others (including Senators Patrick Leahy, D-VT and Kit Bond, R-MO, co-chairs of the Senate National Guard Caucus) introduced S. 215, a bill to "permit each governor to create a homeland security activities plan for the National Guard in his or her State, and authorize the Secretary of Defense to provide oversight and funding for such plans."[19] In her introductory remarks, Senator Feinstein stated that the National Guard is "well-suited to performing an enhanced homeland security mission" for several reasons, including:

- The Guard is already deployed in communities around the country, and integrated into existing local, State, and regional emergency response networks;

- The Guard is responsible for and experienced with homeland security missions, including air sovereignty, disaster relief, and responding to suspected weapons of mass destruction events; and

- The Guard has existing physical, communications, and training infrastructure throughout the United States.[20]

---

[17] 42 U.S.C. 5170 b.
[18] 42 U.S.C. 5170 b (c).
[19] 149 Cong. Rec. S1490, January 23, 2003.
[20] 149 Cong. Rec. S1491, January 23, 2003.

Senator Feinstein also stated that Department of Defense reviews and reports "have made clear that the National Guard should have an expanded role in homeland security."[21]

Although this legislation was not enacted, the issue it addressed—providing an enhanced homeland defense role for the National Guard—was incorporated into a final amendment to Pub.L.No. 108–375, the Ronald W. Reagan National Defense Authorization Act for Fiscal Year 2005. Section 512 of this Act—"Homeland Defense Activities Conducted by the National Guard under Authority of Title 32"—amends Title 32 of the U.S. Code to add a chapter entitled "Homeland Defense Activities" (32 U.S.C. 901 et seq).[22] Section 902 enables the Secretary of Defense to "provide funds to a Governor to employ National Guard units or members to conduct homeland defense activities that the Secretary determines to be necessary and appropriate for participation by the National Guard units or members, as the case may be." Homeland defense activities are defined as activities "undertaken for the military protection of the territory or domestic population of the United States, or of infrastructure or other assets of the United States determined by the Secretary of Defense to be critical to national security, from a threat or aggression against the United States."[23] Governors are authorized to request funding assistance from the Secretary of Defense for the homeland defense activities of the state's National Guard. Requests must include:

- The specific intended homeland defense activities of the National Guard of that State;

- An explanation of why participation of National Guard units or members, as the case may be, in the homeland defense activities is necessary and appropriate; and

- A certification that homeland defense activities are to be conducted at a time when the personnel involved are not in Federal service.[24]

As indicated in the introduction to this report, National Guard members serving in Title 32 status are under the command and control of the state even though the forces are being used for a primary federal purpose and federally funded. According to Major General Timothy Lowenberg, chairman of the Homeland Security Committee of the Adjutants General Association of the United States (AGAUS), the key significance of the 2004 amendment to Title 32 of the U.S. Code is the clarification it provides regarding domestic use of the National Guard.

---

[21] 149 Cong. Rec. S1491, January 23, 2003.
[22] Pub.L.No. 108–375, 118 Stat 1811, 1877, October 28, 2004.
[23] Pub.L.No. 108–375, 118 Stat 1878, 32 U.S.C. 901, 902.
[24] Pub.L.No. 108–375, 118 Stat 1879, 32 U.S.C. 906.

Major General Lowenberg writes that prior to the enactment of Pub.L.No. 108–375, "questions were raised about the statutory authority for Title 32 domestic operations."[25] Title 32 USC, Section 502 (f), adopted in 1964 by Pub.L.No. 88–621, authorizes use of the National Guard at federal expense but under continuing state control "to perform training or other duty."[26] This section of the Code was often interpreted as authorizing training only, and not domestic operations. Major General Lowenberg states that the enactment of 32 U.S.C. 902 resolved "any such ambiguity," and that there is now statutory authority for "use of the Guard under continuing state control but at federal expense, when approved by the Secretary of Defense, for a wide variety of operations, including, when appropriate, protection of oil refineries, nuclear power plants and other critical infrastructure."[27]

Assistant Secretary of Defense for Homeland Defense Paul McHale, testifying before the Commission on the National Guard and Reserves in May 2006, cited the new funding authority given the secretary of defense in 32 U.S.C. 902 as a recognition of

> both the global nature of the current war and the special capabilities and contributions of the National Guard – a military force located in every State and territory, very familiar with the local geography, officials, and population, and well versed in working with other U.S. agencies. Under this authority, National Guard forces can be engaged directly in the defense of the U.S. Homeland in a manner not seen since the days of the Revolutionary War and the War of 1812.[28]

Executive-Branch Documents

In November 1988, President George H.W. Bush issued Executive Order (EO) 12656, "Assignment of Emergency Preparedness Responsibilities." As Amended by EO 13286 in 2003, EO 12656 designates the Department of Homeland Security as the principal agency for coordinating programs and plans among all federal departments, and mandates lead and support responsibilities for each federal agency. As a support responsibility, the secretary of defense is directed to "coordinate with the Secretary of Homeland Security the development of plans for mutual civil-military support during national security emergencies."[29]

---

[25] Lowenberg, 2.
[26] 32 U.S.C. 502 note.
[27] Lowenberg, 2.
[28] Commission on the National Guard and Reserves, *Hearing on Homeland Defense/Homeland Security*, May 3, 2006.
[29] 68 Fed.Reg. 10619, March 5, 2003.

In February 2003, the White House issued Homeland Security Presidential Directive/HSPD–5, the purpose of which is to "enhance the ability of the United States to manage domestic incidents by establishing a single, comprehensive national incident management system."[30] This directive establishes the secretary of homeland defense as the "principal Federal official for domestic incident management," and defines the role of the secretary of defense regarding MSCA:

> The Secretary of Defense shall provide military support to civil authorities for domestic incidents as directed by the President or when consistent with military readiness and appropriate under the circumstances and the law. The Secretary of Defense shall retain command of military forces providing civil support. The Secretary of Defense and the Secretary [of Homeland Security] shall establish appropriate relationships and mechanisms for cooperation and coordination between their two departments.[31]

DEPARTMENT OF DEFENSE REGULATORY DOCUMENTS

Pursuant to the statutes described above, DoD has issued regulatory guidance establishing policies and responsibilities for DoD support of civilian authorities in response to disaster-related civil emergencies and attacks. The department has issued regulations, codified in the Code of Federal Regulations as 32 CFR 185, as well as a series of internal directives that have been re-drafted periodically to reflect changes in both domestic priorities and external threats. DoD Directive No. 3025.1 is the primary directive currently in force that addresses Military Support to Civil Authorities. Prior to its most recent issuance in 1993, it was published in tandem with DoD Directive No. 3025.10, "Military Support of Civil Defense," which has been rescinded. In addition, DoD Directive No. 3025.15, "Military Assistance to Civil Authorities," was issued in 1997 and remains in force. The key provisions of these documents, indicating shifts in policies and responsibilities, are as follows.

DoD Directive Number 3025.1

DoD Directive No. 3025.1 was first issued on January 24, 1952 as Directive No. 200.04–1 pursuant to Pub. L. No. 81–920, the Federal Civil Defense Act of 1950. Its purpose was "to

---

[30] U.S. Office of the President, *Homeland Security Presidential Directive/HSPD–5*, Section (4), February 28, 2003, http://www.whitehouse.gov/news/releases/2003/02/20030228-9.htm.
[31] *Homeland Security Presidential Directive HSPD–5*, Section (9).

establish the responsibilities of the military departments and staff agencies of the Department of Defense for planning and preparations in certain areas of civil defense and related matters."[32] This directive enumerated the responsibilities of the Departments of the Army, Navy, Air Force, Munitions Board, the Research and Development Board, and Joint Chiefs of Staff (JCS). Each service branch was tasked with the development of civil defense programs and policies specific to its operations, and instructed to coordinate with other service branches as well as with the Federal Civil Defense Administration (FCDA), which was authorized by statute to prepare national plans and programs for the civil defense of the United States and delegate civil defense responsibilities to federal departments and agencies.[33] The JCS was given the task of reviewing and coordinating service branch civil defense programs, as well as providing guidance to the FCDA as to "areas which, because of their high importance from the military viewpoint, are considered probable targets for some form of enemy attack and should be given appropriate attention in civil defense planning."[34] In addition, pursuant to Section 302, Pub.L.No. 81–920, during a time of declared civil defense emergency, the Joint Chiefs are directed to formulate DoD recommendations regarding the department's military requirements.

Directive No. 3025.1 was reissued on July 14, 1956, and reprinted with changes through April 23, 1963. The stated purpose of this directive is to establish "Department of Defense policy on the responsibilities of the Assistant Secretary of Defense (Civil Defense), the JCS, and the Military Departments for emergency employment of military resources in domestic emergencies other than civil defense."[35] The term "domestic emergency" is defined to apply to emergencies occurring in the domestic United States, its territories and possessions as a result of "enemy attack, insurrection, civil disturbances, earthquakes, fire, flood, or other public disasters" endangering life and property and disrupting "the usual processes of government."[36] The authorities for this directive are various Executive Orders, as well as Pub.L.No. 81–920 and Pub.L.No. 81–875, which authorized federal agencies, when directed by the president, to provide assistance to states and local governments. Under this directive, the army is given "primary responsibility for coordinating the planning and rendering of military assistance to civil

---

[32] U.S. Department of Defense, Directive Number 200.04–1, January 24, 1952, 1.
[33] Federal Civil Defense Act of 1950, 64 Stat 1248.
[34] DoD Directive No. 200.04–1, 5.
[35] U.S. Department of Defense, Directive No. 3025.1, April 23, 1963, 1. Note that DoD Directive No. 3025.10, issued for the first time on this same date, specifically addresses military support of civil defense.
[36] DoD Directive No. 3025.1, April 23, 1963, Appendix A.

authorities in domestic emergencies."[37] The navy and air force are given diminished responsibility, primarily coordinating their activities with the army. The Joint Chiefs are tasked to issue instructions to commanders regarding emergency military support required in Alaska, Hawaii, and United States possessions and territories. The Assistant Secretary of Defense (Civil Defense) is given specific responsibilities as well:

- Coordinating within the DoD the policy and program aspects of military participation in domestic emergencies and liaison with other Government agencies.

- Providing advice and assistance to DoD agencies and departments on policy aspects of domestic emergency planning.

- Advising the Secretary of Defense on departmental policies and programs relating to domestic emergency matters and occasionally recommending assigned responsibilities for domestic emergency planning.[38]

On November 18, 1965, DoD Directive No. 3025.1 was again resissued and reprinted as amended on April 16, 1971, under the authorities of various Executive Orders and Pub.L.No. 91–606, the Disaster Relief Act of 1970, which enabled the president to direct federal agencies to provide state and local governments with available resources to respond to major disasters. Its purpose was to establish policies, assign responsibilities, and furnish "general guidance" to military departments, the JCS, and other DoD components (referred to collectively as "DoD components") governing the provision of DoD support to civil authorities under natural disaster conditions within the United States, its possessions, and territories.[39] The directive establishes a process whereby the Office of Emergency Preparedness, which was given the authority under executive order to direct and coordinate assistance to state and local governments during major disasters, coordinates with the appropriate military authority to make available necessary personnel, equipment, or other resources. As in earlier directives, the army has primary responsibility for military support, with the navy and air force given supportive, coordinating roles. The JCS assumes the additional responsibility of providing "recommendations to the Secretary of Defense with respect to the planning for and use of military resources for disaster relief operations."[40] The Assistant Secretary for Defense (Administration) is given responsibility for providing guidance and assistance to DoD components and coordinating within the Defense

---

[37] DoD Directive No. 3025.1, April 23, 1963, 3.
[38] DoD Directive No. 3025.1, April 23, 1963, 3.
[39] U.S. Department of Defense, Directive No. 3025.1, April 16, 1971, 1.
[40] DoD Directive No. 3025.1, April 16, 1971, 6.

Department, with respect to policy and program aspects of disaster relief operations and situations.

Directive No. 3025.1 was re-issued later in 1971 (August 30). Many of the provisions remained unchanged, but Directive No. 3025.1 significantly expanded the responsibilities of the army. The secretary of the army was designated the DoD executive agent for military support in disasters. In addition, the Department of the Army was tasked to assign appropriate DoD components the responsibility for supplying necessary resources for disaster relief operations; direct the allocation of committed military resources; conduct liaison with both the Office of Emergency Preparedness and the secretary of defense regarding disaster relief planning and operations; and provide "policy and direction concerning plans, procedures and requirements to all DoD components having cognizance over military resources which may be employed under the provisions of this Directive."[41]

The last re-issuance of Directive No. 3025.1 prior to its current iteration was on May 23, 1980. It establishes as DoD policy the provision of assistance in civil emergencies (defined as "any natural or man-caused emergency, or threat thereof, other than civil defense or wartime emergency, which causes or may cause substantial injury or harm to the population, or substantial property damage or loss.") in accordance with national policies, and consistent with defense priorities.[42] After the president makes a declaration of a major disaster or emergency, the secretary of the army, as DoD executive agent, informs appropriate DoD components. In cases of undeclared civil emergencies warranting national-level response, the decision whether DoD participation is warranted rests with the special assistant to the secretary of defense and deputy secretary of defense in consultation with the DoD executive agent.[43]

The secretary of the army retains the responsibilities mandated in the 1971 directive, with the navy and air force continuing in subordinate roles. The chairman of the JCS is responsible for providing policy guidance and assigning responsibility to subordinate commanders conducting civil emergency relief operations in the United States; advising the DoD executive agent on the planning and use of military resources for civil emergency relief operations; and establishing procedures for transferring military resources assigned to unified and specified commands.[44]

---

[41] DoD Directive No. 3025.1, August 30, 1971, 7.
[42] U.S. Department of Defense, Directive No. 3025.1, May 23, 1980, 2.
[43] DoD Directive No. 3025.1, May 23, 1980, 4.
[44] DoD Directive No. 3025.1, May 23, 1980, 8.

DoD Directive No. 3025.1, issued January 15, 1993, consolidates the policies and responsibilities contained in all previous directives that addressed both disaster-related civil emergencies and attacks on the United States. It creates a "single system for Military Support to Civil Authorities (MSCA) by which DoD components will plan for and respond to requests from civil government agencies" in times of major disasters or emergencies. The authorities for this directive are the Stafford Act (42 U.S.C. 5121 et seq) and the Federal Civil Defense Act of 1950, Pub.L.No. 81–920 (which was repealed in 1994).[45]

In accordance with Pub.L.No. 81–920, a national civil defense policy is mandated, under which the "Department of Defense will support civil authorities in civil defense, to include facilitating the use of the National Guard in each State for response in both peacetime disasters and national security emergencies." The secretary of the army is again designated as the DoD executive agent, in which capacity he develops planning guidance, plans, and procedures for MSCA; tasks DoD components to plan for and commit DoD resources in response to requests from civil authorities; provides guidance (developed with the Joint Chiefs of Staff) to the commanders of the unified and specified commands for MSCA response; and coordinates MSCA plans and procedures with the Federal Emergency Management Administration (FEMA).[46]

The directive establishes, as MSCA policy, that DoD planning is to recognize the following with regard to Army and Air National Guard forces:

- These forces when not in federal service have primary responsibility for providing military assistance to state and local government agencies in civil emergencies.

- Plans and preparedness measures for MSCA must foster close and continuous coordination for efficient employment of DoD resources of the National Guard (under either state or federal authority), as well as resources of the DoD components, in time of peace, war, or transition to war.

- The DoD Components shall augment staffs responsible for MSCA, as appropriate, with personnel from reserve components of all military services who are specifically trained for civil-military planning and emergency liaison duties.

- Military forces employed in MSCA activities shall remain under military command and control of the DoD Executive Agent at all times.[47]

---

[45] U.S. Department of Defense, Directive No. 3025.1, January 15, 1993, 1–2.
[46] DoD Directive No. 3025.1, January 15, 1993, 4–5, 9.
[47] DoD Directive No. 3025.1, January 15, 1993, 6–7.

DoD Directive Number 3025.10

As noted earlier in this report, beginning April 1963 the U.S. Department of Defense, under authority of Pub.L. No. 81–920, issued Directive No. 3025.10, which addressed only military support of civil defense under a national emergency involving an attack, or a condition that might precede an attack, on the United States. It was issued again in March 1965 and July 1981, and cancelled by DoD Directive No. 3025.1 in January 1993.

Whereas Directive No. 3025.1 assigns primary responsibilities for implementation of DoD policy to the secretary of the army as DoD executive agent, Directive No. 3025.10 tasks the JCS with "overall responsibility for providing military support of civil defense," and suspends the executive agent responsibilities of the secretary of the army.[48] The directive stipulates that subject to JCS approval, the military services and defense agencies are to "make available to state or local authorities during a civil defense emergency those resources not otherwise committed to current or planned military operations or to other priority missions" cited elsewhere in this directive.[49] The directive also stipulates that "military forces, active and reserve, and the National Guard when federalized, shall be considered potentially available to provide military support of civil defense to civil authorities during a civil defense emergency."[50]

DoD Directive Number 3025.15

DoD Directive No. 3025.15, issued on February 18, 1997, and still in force, establishes DoD policy and assigns responsibilities for providing military assistance to civil authorities, including DoD responses to civil emergencies under DoD Directive No. 3025.1.

All requests by civil authorities for DoD military assistance must be evaluated by "DoD approval authorities" against several criteria. The secretary of the army is designated approval authority for "emergency support in response to natural or man-made disasters."[51] The secretary of defense has approval authority for support to civil authorities involving:

- Use of commander in chief–assigned forces;

- DoD support to civil disturbances;

---

[48] U.S. Department of Defense, Directive No. 3025.10, July 21, 1981, 2–3.
[49] DoD Directive No. 3025.10, July 21, 1981, 3.
[50] DoD Directive No. 3025.10, July 21, 1981, 3.
[51] U.S. Department of Defense, Directive No. 3025.15, February 18, 1997, 3.

- DoD responses to acts of terrorism; and

- DoD support in potentially confrontational planned events involving specifically identified persons and/or groups.[52]

The criteria that must be applied by both approval authorities are:

- Legality (compliance with laws);

- Lethality (potential use of lethal force by or against DoD Forces);

- Risk (safety of DoD Forces);

- Cost (who pays, and impact on DoD budget);

- Appropriateness (whether the requested mission is in the interest of the Department to conduct); and

- Readiness (impact on Defense's ability to perform its primary mission).[53]

Department of Defense Regulations

Title 32, Part 185 of the Code of Federal Regulations, currently entitled Military Support to Civil Authorities, was initially promulgated in 1965, and again in 1981, under authority of Pub.L.No. 81–920, and entitled Military Support of Civil Defense. The 1965 and 1981 regulations complement DoD Directive No. 3025.10, as they address Defense Department policies and assign responsibilities for the provision of "military support of civil defense under a national emergency involving an attack [the descriptive 'nuclear' was deleted in 1981], or a condition that might precede an attack, on the United States."[54] The primary responsibilities of the JCS are set forth in identical language as that of DoD Directive 3025.10. Similarly, the text of 12 CFR 185, as adopted on October 12, 1993 (58 FR 52667) is identical to that of DoD Directive 3025.1 issued January 15, 1993.

NATIONAL RESPONSE PLAN/DEFENSE STRATEGY DOCUMENT

The September 11, 2001, attacks on the United States led to the establishment of a homeland security infrastructure and prompted the issuance of numerous homeland security presidential directives. The issuance was followed by the development of comprehensive

---

[52] DoD Directive No. 3025.15, 3
[53] DoD Directive No. 3025.15, 3.
[54] 30 Fed.Reg. 4753, April 14, 1965 and 46 Fed.Reg. 48189, October 1, 1981.

homeland security strategies by the Department of Defense and Department of Homeland Security. It is within this broad framework that administration policy regarding MSCA is being developed.

In December 2004, the Department of Homeland Security adopted a new *National Response Plan*, the purpose of which is to "establish a comprehensive, national, all-hazards approach to domestic incident management across a spectrum of activities including prevention, preparedness, response, and recovery."[55] Pursuant to directive HSPD–5, the secretary of homeland security is the principal federal official for domestic incident management and declares "incidents of national significance" in situations where specific criteria have been met, including the inability of state and local governments to adequately respond to major disasters or emergencies and catastrophic incidents. The plan stipulates that the Defense Department's role in the federal response to these incidents is to provide "defense support of civil authorities for domestic incidents as directed by the President or when consistent with military readiness and appropriate under the circumstances and the law. The Secretary of Defense shall retain command of military forces providing civil support." Domestic incidents include terrorist attacks, major disasters, and other emergencies.[56]

In June 2005, the Department of Defense issued its *Strategy for Homeland Defense and Civil Support*, which reiterates the department's role of providing support to civil authorities at the direction of the president or secretary of defense. This document states that "the National Guard is particularly well suited for civil support missions" and that reserve forces "currently provide many key homeland defense and civil support capabilities, including intelligence, military police, medical expertise, and chemical decontamination." However, the Defense Department believes that "the nation needs to focus particular attention on better using the competencies of National Guard and Reserve Component organizations," and recommends "the most promising areas for employment of the National Guard and Reserve forces: air and missile defense; maritime security; land defense; CBRNE response; and critical infrastructure protection."[57]

---

[55] *National Response Plan*, 2.
[56] *National Response Plan*, 10, 41.
[57] *Strategy for Homeland Defense and Civil Support*, 35–36.

DEPARTMENT OF DEFENSE CIVILIAN AND MILITARY RESPONSIBILITY FOR MSCA

The directives and regulations enumerated earlier in this report, all of which were adopted prior to the September 11 attacks, assign specific responsibilities for MSCA implementation and coordination to various assistant secretaries. In November 2002, Congress enacted legislation—Pub.L.No. 107–314, the Bob Stump National Defense Authorization Act for Fiscal Year 2003—that mandated the appointment of a new assistant secretary for homeland defense—ASD(HD)—whose principal duty is the overall supervision of the homeland defense activities of the Department of Defense.[58] Paul McHale was named to this position in 2003. According to the DoD's 2005 homeland defense/civil support strategy document, the establishment of this position "responded to the need for improved policy guidance to DoD Components on homeland defense and civil support issues."[59] The department's Web site further describes the ASD(HD) responsibilities:

> under the authority, direction and control of the Under Secretary of Defense for Policy, and, as appropriate, in coordination with the Chairman of the Joint Chiefs of Staff, the ASD(HD) provides oversight to DoD homeland defense activities, develops policies, conducts analyses, provides advice, and makes recommendations on homeland defense, **defense support of civil authorities** [emphasis added], emergency preparedness and domestic crisis management matters within the Department. Specifically, the ASD(HD) assists the Secretary of Defense in providing policy direction on homeland defense matters through the Chairman of the Joint Chiefs of Staff to the United States Northern Command and other Combatant/commands, as applicable, to guide the development and execution of their plans and duties.[60]

According to the Defense Department's 2005 homeland security doctrine, in 2003 the secretary of defense vested the roles and responsibilities associated with the DOD executive agent for MSCA and MACDIS (Military Assistance for Civil Disturbances) with the assistant secretary for homeland defense. Pursuant to department directives, the secretary of the army had previously been designated DOD executive agent. The doctrine further states that in March 2003,

> the roles and responsibilities associated with the DOD Executive Agent for MSCA and MACDIS were rescinded. ASD(HD) was subsequently assigned the

---

[58] Pub.L.No. 107–314, 116 Stat 2458, December 2, 2002.
[59] *Strategy for Homeland Defense and Civil Support*, 8.
[60] U.S. Department of Defense, Office of the Assistant Secretary of Defense for Homeland Defense and America's Security Affairs, "FAQ's: Homeland Defense," http://www.defenselink.mil/policy/sections/policy_offices/hd/faqs/homelandDefense/index.html.

responsibility for the support within DOD. The Secretary of Defense (SecDef) also transferred the functions and associated resources of the Army's Office of the Director of Military Support to the Joint Chiefs of Staff office of the Joint Director of Military Support (JDOMS). Guidance from SecDef or the ASD(HD) is translated into operational orders developed by JDOMS. JDOMS produces military orders as they pertain to domestic emergencies, forwards them to SecDef for approval and then to the appropriate military commander for execution.[61]

The classified Unified Command Plan (UCP) establishes the missions and responsibilities of each combatant command within the armed forces. As authorized by President George W. Bush on April 17, 2002, the Department of Defense announced changes to the UCP, effective October 1, 2002, including the establishment of the U.S. Northern Command (USNORTHCOM) "to consolidate under a single unified command those existing homeland defense and civil support missions that were previously executed by other military organizations."[62] With regard to MSCA, USNORTHCOM defines its specific mission: "As directed by the president or secretary of defense, provide defense support of civil authorities including consequence management operations."[63] Assistant Secretary for Homeland Defense Paul McHale, testifying in May 2006, stated that one of the improvements DoD was implementing to better respond to future catastrophes like Hurricane Katrina was the formulation of a "contingency plan defining USNORTHCOM's role in planning and executing support to the Department of Homeland Security (DHS) during domestic contingencies."[64]

STATES' ROLE IN MSCA

The states' governors are commanders in chief of the National Guard when serving in their respective states. The National Guard is the only military force available to governors in times of disasters and emergencies, or for enforcement use such as airport and border security following the attacks of September 11, 2001. The National Governors Association (NGA) has taken a very active role in representing the states' position regarding the National Guard's role in support of civil authorities. The NGA's current Army and Air National Guard Policy, which is subject to amendment at the association's February 2007 winter meeting, affirms that the "states and territories have an enormous stake in the ongoing effectiveness and efficiency of their

---

[61] *Homeland Security*, IV–10.
[62] "U.S. Northern Command: History," http://www.northcom.mil/about_us/history.htm.
[63] "U.S. Northern Command," http://www.northcom.mil/about_us/about_us.htm.

National Guard."[65] In particular, the governors believe that the National Guard "can be an effective force multiplier to civil authorities in responding to terrorism at the state, local, and federal levels." The governors urge DoD to reaffirm the National Guard's activities to secure strategic facilities "as an integral part of the ongoing mission of the National Guard," and ensure that sufficient funding and training is provided to enable the Guard to meet the responsibilities of the current homeland defense environment.[66]

In their policy statement, the governors also express support for the amendments to Title 32 USC adopted in 2004 regarding deployment of the National Guard for homeland defense activities, and believe that National Guard domestic missions should generally be performed in Title 32 status rather than Title 10 status. They also state that they agree with the U.S. Government Accountability Office's November 2004 recommendation that "the Secretary of Defense develop and submit a strategy to Congress for improving the Army National Guard's structure and readiness and clearly define the Guard's role in homeland defense and providing support to civilian authorities."[67]

ROLE OF DOD IN DOMESTIC DEFENSE

As DoD policy and congressional intent regarding MSCA have evolved over time, the consistent emphasis has been on the *supportive* nature of DoD's role vis-à-vis the states, and the supremacy of military operations abroad. In light of the September 11, 2001, homeland attacks and the development of new defense and homeland security strategies, questions have been raised as to whether or not homeland defense should now be a primary mission, or even the primary mission, of the military, specifically the National Guard.

The DoD internal directives are clear in stipulating that in the event of a natural disaster or other domestic emergency, state resources must be overwhelmed or exhausted as a precondition to providing federal military resources. In addition, non-MSCA military operations take precedence. As far back as 1952, DoD stipulated that the army was to be responsible for emergency military support of civil defense operations "wherein the civil defense organizations

---

[64] *Hearing on Homeland Defense/Homeland Security.*
[65] National Governors Association, *Policy Position HHS–03: Army and Air National Guard*, February 27, 2004, 3.1, http://www.nga.org.
[66] National Governors Association, *Policy Position HHS–03*, 3.4.
[67] National Governors Association, *Policy Position HHS–03*, 3.4.

[of state and local governments] are unprepared or otherwise incapable of operating without their support."[68] DoD Directive No. 3025.1 currently in force states as policy that DoD resources are provided "only when response or recovery requirements are beyond the capabilities of civil authorities," and also that, unless directed by the secretary of defense, "military operations other than MSCA will have priority over MSCA."[69]

DoD's 2005 homeland security doctrine also addresses the military's civil support function, tasking military commanders to ensure that DoD resources are used judiciously by providing these resources "only when response or recovery requirements are beyond the capabilities of local, state, and federal authorities, and when they are requested by an LFA [Lead Federal Agency] and approved by the Secretary of Defense." The LFA should only request DoD assistance when "other local, state, and federal capabilities have been exhausted or when a military-unique capability is required."[70] This "resource of last resort" role for DoD is echoed in the Defense Department's 2005 *Strategy for Homeland Defense and Civil Support* and the Department of Homeland Security's *National Response Plan*, which also affirms that non-MSCA military activities are paramount: "Defense support of civil authorities is provided when local, State, and Federal resources are overwhelmed, provided that it does not interfere with the Department's military readiness or operations."[71]

Witnesses have testified on behalf of the Department of Defense and the Department of Homeland Security before various congressional committees and the Commission on the National Guard and Reserves (CNGR) regarding the Defense Department's homeland defense mission. Their testimony offers some indication of the future role the department will play, but their statements are often contradictory or vague. For example, at a December 2006 hearing before the CNGR, Dr. David Chu, Under Secretary of Defense for Personnel and Readiness, was asked to what extent the nation should rely on the National Guard for the performance of Civil Support missions. He replied:

> We should not see the Guard as a unique asset for homeland support missions,
> and we saw in fact the opposite in Katrina. Let's not particularize this mission to
> the National Guard; let's use all elements of national strength in responding to

---

[68] DoD Directive No. 3025.1, January 24, 1952, 2.
[69] DoD Directive No. 3025.1, Janaury 15, 1993, 6.
[70] *Homeland Security*, IV–1 and IV–4.
[71] *National Response Plan*, 42.

any particular homeland crisis or difficulty we face, and in our judgment that includes other federal agencies.[72]

At that same hearing, George Foresman, Under Secretary for Preparedness, Department of Homeland Security, argued initially for a diminished role for the National Guard, but in his conclusion, appeared to take an opposite view. He stated that the United States has

> the capacity to prevent, protect, and respond and recover domestically across a wide range of hazards and threats that form our risk continuum, While the military (whether we are talking about active, reserve, or National Guard), are going to be important components, they should not be foundational components. On the whole we should be looking to increase the capabilities of our civilian community so that we lessen the reliance on the military community for the traditional military support to civil authorities.

He later concluded by saying that

> we must recognize that in today's Homeland Security environment characterized by asymmetrical threats, i.e, natural disasters, as well as the threat of terrorism, the National Guard must be capable of responding to support States when called upon and Federal actions when required. The National Guard must be dual-hatted for either a domestic civil support role or a war time operations role in a way that keeps them ready and vigilant.[73]

Assistant Secretary for Homeland Defense Paul McHale was not consistent is his testimony, either. In 2003, shortly after he assumed his new post, he testified before a congressional hearing on the role of the department and the National Guard in homeland security, at which time he affirmed unequivocally the supportive relationship DoD has with respect to DHS:

> When we provide support to civilian agencies, it is indeed just that. The civilian agency in the United States will under all circumstances take the lead. We will provide support as appropriate. The military chain of command throughout that process will be preserved. There are no assigned forces in the Department of Homeland Security. The military chain of command goes from President of the United States to the Secretary of Defense to the Combatant Commander who is tasked with the responsibility. But we will support upon order of the President those activities where the capabilities of the Department of Defense may be unique in that they don't exist within the civilian sector or under extraordinary circumstances where civilian authorities may be overwhelmed by the magnitude of the task. When it comes to military activity in the United States in a civil

---

[72] Commission on the National Guard and Reserves, *Hearing on Proposed Changes to National Guard*, December 13–14, 2006.
[73] *Hearing on Proposed Changes to National Guard*, December 13, 2006.

support role, we are not the lead Federal agency. It is only when a civilian agency is unable to address a challenge at hand that DOD capabilities would be brought into play.[74]

In that same prepared statement, McHale commented on the role of the National Guard, stating that, on the one hand, it will be necessary for the Guard to continue to provide "the strategic reserve with regard to overseas combat," but that "consistent with its force structure and end strength, we will see an enhanced homeland defense mission for the National Guard. The National Guard can play an extremely important role, in fact perhaps a central role in responding to those threats that manifest themselves within the United States."[75]

In March 2006 testimony before the U.S. Senate, McHale reaffirmed this enhanced role for the National Guard, citing the statutory authority given the Defense Department in 2004 to fund use of the Guard for approved homeland defense activities. He stated that "under this authority, National Guard forces will be engaged directly in the defense of the U.S. in a manner not seen since the early days of our country." At that same hearing, he stated that in the global conflict in which the United States is engaged, "the defense of the U.S. homeland is the preeminent duty [of DoD]." He later cited the statutory authority for the Department of Homeland Security's responsibility to secure borders and all transportation systems as well as prevent the entry of terrorists into the United States, noting that DoD's "role in the execution of this responsibility is to provide *support* [emphasis added] to DHS, when requested, appropriate, lawful, and approved by the President or Secretary of Defense."[76] As to the balance between the mission here and that abroad, he noted in his discussion of how DoD provides defense support to civil authorities (DSCA) that "DoD has continued its long tradition of DSCA while maintaining its primary mission of fighting and winning the nation's wars."[77]

Major General Timothy Lowenberg, who over the past few years has staunchly advocated the position that the National Guard is vital to national defense and homeland security, gave testimony in 2003 on behalf of AGAUS that illustrates why, despite all the arguments for

[74] U.S. Congress, House of Representatives, Committee on Armed Services, Subcommittee on Terrorism, Unconventional Threats and Capabilities, *Hearing on National Defense Authorization Act for Fiscal Year 2004—H.R. 1588—and Oversight of Previously Authorized Programs*, 108th Cong., 1st sess., March 13, 2003, 5.

[75] *Hearing on National Defense Authorization Act for Fiscal Year 2004*, 5–6.

[76] U.S. Congress, Senate Committee on Armed Services, Subcommittee on Emerging Threats and Capabilities, *Roles and Missions of the Department of Defense Regarding Homeland Defense and Support to Civil Authorities*, March 10, 2006.

[77] *Roles and Missions of the Department of Defense*, March 10, 2006.

increased homeland security, the military remains unwilling to perceive its MSCA function as paramount. Major General Lowenberg testified that both the AGAUS and the National Guard Association of the United States

> urge the President to direct the Secretary of Defense, and request the Congress where necessary, to authorize, support, equip and fund the National Guard to assume significant homeland security responsibilities. These responsibilities must be recognized as *an* important mission but not *the* sole or primary mission of the National Guard. Although there may be a need for selected units and personnel to be specially missioned or resourced for these purposes, homeland security can most effectively and efficiently be accomplished as a *dual mission* that compliments, enhances and draws its essential strength from the National Guard's continued combat force structure, training, and experience.[78]

In 2006 the Center for Strategic and International Studies (CSIS) released a report on the future of the National Guard and Reserves, in which it addressed the use of these DoD components to protect the U.S. homeland. The report notes that "almost five years after the September 11 attacks, it is still not clear how the Reserve Component should organize, train and equip for homeland defense and civil support, and what priority it should place on these missions."[79] The report concludes that despite the September 11 attacks, "DoD's fundamental emphasis continues to be 'the away game.'"[80] This is illustrated by the definition of MSCA contained in the department's 2005 homeland security strategy (cited extensively throughout this report) and statements made at congressional hearings. In particular, the report notes USNORTHCOM Deputy Commander Inge's March 2006 Senate testimony that USNORTHCOM is responsible for homeland defense and focused every day on "deterring, preventing and defeating attacks against our homeland." USNORTHCOM "stands ready to assist primary agencies in responding quickly to man-made and natural disasters, when directed by the President or Secretary of Defense."[81] According to CSIS,

> close observers know that [General Inge's] words telegraph DoD's fundamental approach to civil support – the military will provide response capabilities if asked, but it does not envision its support on a wide scale, it will not make civil support missions a priority for significant forces on a consistent basis, and it will not take an activist approach to determining requirements for the civil support mission.[82]

---

[78] *Hearing on National Defense Authorization Act for Fiscal Year 2004,* 78.
[79] Wormuth, 63.
[80] Wormuth, 64.
[81] *Roles and Missions of the Department of Defense*, March 10, 2006.
[82] Wormuth, 64.

It is also of note that in February 2001, the United States Commission on National Security (also known as the Hart–Rudman Commission) was tasked to "review in a comprehensive way U.S. national security requirements for the next century."[83] Although the commission recommended various enhanced capabilities for the National Guard in order that it become "a critical asset for homeland security," its overall recommendation was that "the Secretary of Defense, at the President's direction, should make homeland security *a* [emphasis added] primary mission of the National Guard, and the Guard should be organized, properly trained, and adequately equipped to undertake that mission."[84] CSIS views this language as a "nod to the military's well-known resistance to putting homeland defense and civil support on an equal footing with other military missions."[85]

CONCLUSION

Although the U.S. military has been authorized to provide support to civil authorities in response to major disasters and emergencies since 1951, since September 11, 2001, this function is significantly changed in scope and importance. For example, highly trained army and marine corps units are positioned to respond to a wide range of threats to the United States, including critical infrastructure protection; the U.S. Marine Corps Chemical-Biological Incident Response Force can be deployed to assist local, state, or federal agencies and military commanders in consequence management operations by providing capabilities for detection and stabilization of contaminated personnel; and Joint Task Force Civil Support is trained to provide critical life support during a CBRNE situation in the United States.[86]

The Department of Defense currently views protecting the U.S. homeland from attack as its highest priority.[87] In order to "prevent, prepare for, respond to, and recover from terrorist attacks, major disasters, and other emergencies, the United States government" has established a single, comprehensive approach to domestic incident management and designated the secretary of homeland security as the principal federal official for domestic incident management.[88] The

---

[83] U.S. Commission on National Security/21st Century, *Road Map for National Security: Imperative for Change*, Phase III Report (April 2000-February 2001), February 15, 2001, 26, http://www.au.af.mil/au/awc/awcgate/nssg.
[84] *Road Map for National Security*, 25.
[85] Wormuth, 64.
[86] *Roles and Missions of the Department of Defense*, March 10, 2006.
[87] *Strategy for Homeland Defense and Civil Support*, 1.
[88] *HSPD–5*, (4).

creation of a homeland security infrastructure has been followed by a myriad of doctrines, strategies, and directives from the White House, Department of Homeland Security, and Department of Defense. It is within the framework of this new body of policy that MSCA is being defined. The regulations and DoD directives currently in force that govern MSCA predate the threats of the twenty-first century, and likely will be amended.

Although definitions of MSCA can be found throughout the new wave of official homeland security documents, the larger question of the primacy of this mission is often raised, but never clearly answered. Should MSCA be *a* primary mission for the mission for the military? *The* primary mission? Congress has addressed the issue of the role of the Defense Department and the National Guard in homeland defense at annual hearings on the National Defense Authorization Act, and the Commission on the National Guard and Reserves has held extensive hearings on this topic as well. Testimony given at these hearings by officials from the Department of Homeland Security and the Department of Defense, particularly Assistant Secretary for Homeland Defense Paul McHale, always begins with language on the unequivocal importance of homeland defense, followed by the immediate disclaimer that DHS is the lead federal agency, with DoD providing support, as appropriate, and at the direction of the president and secretary of defense. The suggestion has even been made that civilian capabilities should be enhanced to address the consequences of disasters like Hurricane Katrina, thereby lessening the burden on the military. In addition, although witnesses attest to the long history of MSCA as a military function, they are quick to state that DoD's primary mission is fighting and winning the nation's wars.

In sum, it can be said that DoD policy with regard to Military Support to Civil Authorities is a work in progress because of the escalating importance of homeland defense. However, based on statements by department officials directly responsible for the MSCA function, it would seem unlikely that future statements of policy, e.g., regulations and directives, will place homeland defense and civil support on an equal footing with military missions abroad.

BIBLIOGRAPHY

Blum, H. Steven. "A Vision for the National Guard." *Joint Force Quarterly*, no. 36 (2003).

Commission on the National Guard and Reserves. *Hearing on Homeland Defense/Homeland Security*. May 3, 2006. http://www.cngr.gov/public-hearings-events.asp.

Commission on the National Guard and Reserves. *Hearing on Proposed Changes to National Guard*. December 13–14, 2006. http://www.cngr.gov/public-hearings-events.asp.

Lowenberg, Timothy J. "The Role of the National Guard in National Defense and Homeland Security." *National Guard*, September 1, 2005. http://www.ngaus.org.

National Defense Panel. *Transforming Defense: National Security in the 21st Century*. December 1997. http://www.dtic.mil/ndp/FullDoc2.pdf.

Preiss, Robert A. "The National Guard and Homeland Defense." *Joint Force Quarterly*, no. 36 (2003).

U.S. Army War College. *How the Army Runs (HTAR)*. 25th ed. Carlisle, PA: October 2006. http://www.carlisle.army.mil/usawc/dclm/htar2005.htm.

U.S. Commission on National Security/21st Century. *Road Map for National Security: Imperative for Change*. Phase III Report (April 2000–February 2001). February 15, 2001. http://www.au.af.mil/au/awc/awcgate/nssg.

U.S. Congress. House of Representatives. Committee on Armed Services. Subcommittee on Terrorism, Unconventional Threats and Capabilities. *Hearing on National Defense Authorization Act for Fiscal Year 2004 – H.R. 1588 – and Oversight of Previously Authorized Programs*. 108th Cong., 1st sess., March 13, 19, 27, April 1, 3, 2003.

U.S. Congress. House of Representatives. Committee on Government Reform. *Transforming the National Guard: Resourcing for Readiness*. 108th Cong., 2d sess., April 29, 2004.

U.S. Congress. Senate. Committee on Armed Services. Subcommittee on Emerging Threats and Capabilities. *The Roles and Missions of the Department of Defense Regarding Homeland Defense and Support to Civil Authorities in Review of the Defense Authorization Request for Fiscal Year 2007 and the Future Years Defense Program*. 109th Cong., 2d sess., March 10, 2006.

U.S. Department of Defense. *Strategy for Homeland Defense and Civil Support*. Washington, DC: June 2005. http://www.defenselink.mil/news/Jun2005/d20050630homeland.pdf.

U.S. Department of Homeland Security. *National Response Plan*. December 2004. http://www.dhs.gov/xlibrary/assets/NRP_FullText.pdf.

U.S. Government Accountability Office. *DOD Needs to Assess the Structure of U.S. Forces for Domestic Military Missions*. GAO–03–670. July 2003. http://www.gao.gov.

U.S. Joint Chiefs of Staff. *Homeland Security*. Joint Publication 3–26. August 2, 2005. http://www.dtic.mil/doctrin/jel/new_pubs/jp3_26.pdf.

U.S. Library of Congress. Congressional Research Service. *Hurricane Katrina: DOD Disaster Response*. RL33095, Washington, DC, September 19, 2005.

Wormuth, Christine E. *The Future of the National Guard and Reserves: The Beyond Goldwater-Nichols Phase III Report*. Washington, DC: Center for Strategic and International Studies, July 2006. http://www.csis.org/media/csis/pubs/bgn_ph3_report.pdf.

Also used in the preparation of this report were the U.S. Code, the Code of Federal Regulations, and U.S. Department of Defense directives; those directives that are currently in force are available at http://dtic.mil/wh/directives. The author also consulted the Office of the President Web site for presidential directives (http://www.whitehouse.gov) and the Web site of USNORTHCOM and its Joint Task Force Civil Support for history and mission statement (http://www.northcom.mil and http://jtfcs.northcom.mil).